Principles of the Jewish Wealth

Understanding the Principles of the Jewish Wealth

James A Lynch

ISBN 10 - 1450589340 ISBN 13 - 9781450589345

The Principles of the Jewish Wealth have been deliberately hidden for almost four thousand years. Why? To hide them from the lazy and the wicked. Every person in their right and conscious mind has the ability to attain wealth.

Dedication

This book is dedicated to my wonderful wife, Lisa, who has supported and encouraged me through the good times and the challenging times

Contents

Introduction

Principles of the Jewish wealth

Introduction

Have you ever seen or heard of a poor Jewish person? The very term Jew instills a confident background of wealth and prosperity. The richest people on record in all of history are Jews.

The Jewish language is a difficult language to learn in that it has a lot more expression and description than, for example, the English language. But to have somebody explain and teach the element of wealth built into the Jewish culture, the understanding that a Jew is destined and expected to be wealthy and the underlying confidence of attaining enormous political, social, business and monetary wealth is the most extraordinary journey you can ever travel.

To compress the heritage, upbringing and lifestyle of the entire Jewish wealth system into one book would be almost impossible, but what I have attempted to do is explain my wealth - how I, as a middle class Australian was taught how to become wealthy - and to introduce you to the principles and base elements of the Jewish wealth system so that you will begin your ongoing study.

I was originally introduced to principles of the Jewish wealth system by the wealthy assistant of an old Jew. This wealthy assistant eventually introduced me to the old Jew Himself who has since taken me in, as his assistant, as His protégé. I am now exceedingly, abundantly wealthy and I still work the principles to my advantage every day.

Principles of the Jewish wealth

Learning how to live

People often say if only life had an instruction manual. I can assure you, one has been written. It is a secret, written in the culture and upbringing of the Jewish people.

The Jewish people understand the principles of attaining and maintaining wealth. It is taught to them from a very young age. It is a part of their heritage. In the Jewish culture it is deliberately instilled in them as part of their upbringing.

No other culture has such a long history of deliberately attaining and maintaining wealth.

There are rules and laws to uphold to bring wealth into your life. The Jewish people have a written law; a long, decisive and very old book containing this written law, including the principles and a step by step guide that does not fail to bring wealth into your life if it is strictly obeyed. Let me repeat that - if it is obeyed.

Before being introduced to the principles of the Jewish wealth, I read as many books as I could on becoming wealthy. I read many books on investing, on trading and on being successful.

The thing I have learned is that most of these books were right on track, most of them had the traits and the background of what I have since been taught. Many of them formed a backbone that has only been strengthened by what I have learned. They taught that you must watch what you say (in that you speak positively), act in a manner that is becoming of what you are becoming and that you deal honestly, fairly and with integrity.

First things First: The First Principle

The first principle I was taught is that I must be a giver. I must give. This was not new to me at all; I had already read that many large corporations understand the subliminal and unseen forces that work to their direct advantage when they give to charities and other organizations in need of help. Start taking note of how often you read and hear of the donations companies and individuals give and remember, this is only the donations you hear about, most don't publicize their giving or the amount they give.

According to the Jewish law it is prohibited to take a vow of poverty. This is a very strict part of the law. Other parts of the Jewish law and the requirements of it require you to have enough money to take care of yourself, your family and to be wealthy enough to leave an inheritance to your grandchildren. On top of this you are required to have enough money to take care of others.

To quote my friend, the old Jew Himself, you are to have enough for yourself, your family and for every charitable donation! In other words, you are to have enough for what you want and enough to look after other people.

Guidelines to Giving

The Jewish law has strict guidelines to giving. The Jew must give away the first ten percent of what he/she earns. Let's just stop there and think about the importance of that statement. The first ten percent of what he earns, not just ten percent. In other words we are putting more importance on our money we give away than on paying bills. This idea may be hard to swallow at first but, until you realise and understand the importance of giving, then you will understand the importance of giving first, then paying the bills, the mortgage and so on. This will ensure that you are in control of your money and that your money is not in control of you.

Who do you give to? This is just as important as giving itself. The Jewish law lists several groups and organisations you are to give to. For starters it says that you are to have enough for every charitable donation. Charity, or giving, is to some degree one in the same. You are to give to charities but not just charities. You are also to keep a look out and give to the widow, the fatherless and the poor. However, not just any poor person or organisation. We will look in more detail at exactly who and who not to give to but on the subject of who not to give to; you don't give to people who just won't work, not to people who are just lazy; you are to help those who are trying to help themselves. Another way of saying this is to explain the difference of giving a poor person money or giving them, for example, a chicken. If you just give a poor person money then you are funding their poverty and simply bank rolling them to the next hand-out.

But if you give them a chicken, and teach them to sell eggs, raise chicks, build up a flock of more chickens and sell more eggs until they are no longer poor, then you are sowing your money into better soil than if you just give a poor person money.

The government gives poor people money every day, from local welfare to world aid. The result, in most cases, is that the poor person learns to line up at the welfare office the following fortnight for more money instead of learning how to generate an income for himself and get off the welfare system. He learns to rely on that system instead of learning to rely on the system of generating money, giving back ten percent to those in need and investing or re-working the remaining profit.

So exactly who do you give to?

Sow seed into good soil

The Jewish law often relates to and gives examples of a farmer.

The farmer goes out into the field and sows seed. He sows diligently; he does not just throw his seed out the back door, say "I've sown my seed" and hope for a great crop and a bumper harvest.

Instead, he looks for the best soil in which to sow his seed, which he has already invested in by having to get his hands on that seed in the first place so he takes care as to where he sows it. Why? Because he is expecting a return on his investment.

He searches for the best ground, the most fertile soil, he prepares the ground, he protects the ground and he is careful about where he sows his seed.

The law describes how much return to expect. The amount of money you receive back is directly proportional to how much you give, in proportion to what you earn and where you give it. Another way of saying that is where you sow it or the quality of the ground in which you sow your seed, and how much seed you sow, will determine the quality of the harvest you get.

Getting back to the farmer it says that when the farmer sows seed, some seed falls on good ground, some falls on stony ground. The seed that falls on good ground can yield a harvest of up to one hundred times of that which was sown, the seed that falls on the stony ground may only bring in a small harvest if any at all. This is a typical farming expectation.

What this is saying is that you must have diligence as to where you give, you cannot be a lazy giver and expect a good return on what you give, you need to do your due diligence and research on the charity or the people that you are giving to. You are to treat it like any other investment. You don't just give to the first charity you find and say "I've given to my charity, show me the return".

When you give, ten percent of your income is the minimum you are to give away; this is a strict part of the law and written in a strict legal format.

You cannot be a lazy giver and expect a good return on what you give, you need to do your due diligence and research on the charity or the people that you are giving to.

Expecting a return

A farmer expects a return on the seed he sows. He expects to get a lot more back as a harvest than what he has sown into the ground. If he does not get anything back, or if he only gets back what he has sown, then it was not worth farming in the first place. The same is to be said when giving to a charity. So many people have a problem when giving with an expectation to receive. Think along the same lines as any other investment, knowing the principles and believing in what you are doing, expect a good result. Learn to expect; expect a good result. Expect a return on your giving and just keep giving, just keep sowing your seeds.

Examine the way that you speak in all areas of your life. I mentioned earlier about the power of positive thinking and, just as importantly, the power of positive speech. I'll cover this in more depth, but treat your donations as you would any other venture - think well of it, speak well of it and expect well of it.

Expect a return on your giving and just keep giving, just keep sowing your seeds.

Principles of the Jewish wealth

Where does the return come from?

When I began teaching people the principles of the Jewish wealth system, it was not hard to teach most people to give. It was much harder to teach them that they were to expect a return on their money. The first thing they would say is that surely you are not telling me to give to receive! That was just too much for them to handle. The fact is that when you give, you will receive. When you learn that it is a universal principle of the unseen realm, then you will learn to work it to your advantage. Even better still, in most countries, Australia included, giving a donation to the larger organisations, in most cases, is tax deductible.

The Jewish law indicates to expect to receive a return on your charity giving. It also describes exactly how much to expect to receive and when to expect it. Let's go again and look at the farmer, look at the other side of the pendulum, the natural world.

When a farmer goes out to his field to sow corn, he sows corn seeds and corn grows. But he does not just get back one grain of corn, he get back many corn stalks. Every corn stalk has many corn seeds inside of it. Nobody would go out and sow with the expectation of just getting back the same amount that he gave into the ground. But he goes out and sows with an expectation of getting a harvest many times that of which he sowed in the first place. What then? Then he takes the first ten percent and sows that the next season for another harvest. The Jewish law states that we are to expect a return on what we give of between thirty times and one hundred times that which we have given.

When I tell people to expect back one hundred times more than what they gave, they almost choke. But when we look at nature, a hundred-fold return on seed sown in the ground is not unreasonable at all. In fact if you sow a kernel or corn seed, when that corn grows up and you pick that full ear of corn and tear it open, without doubt you are expecting a full head of corn! You would never expect only to have a couple or just one little corn seed there on your corn cob.

Where did you sow that corn seed? You carefully chose a spot in the garden that would best suit growing corn. You looked for, or even bought and had delivered the best soil to your vegetable patch. You spent money on the ground before you even spent money on the seed. You prepared the ground, you created an environment that would best suit the seed you are about to sow. You then sowed the seed but you didn't stop there. You put snail bait around the seedling as it grew to stop the snails eating it, you checked on it regularly. You added some fertiliser if it needed it. You watered that seed regularly as it needed it and best of all you watched it grow. As importantly, you spoke well of it, you probably even spoke to it.

You must now take a moment to stop and realize that the process does not stop there. You don't come this far just to watch the corn grow. You then harvest that corn. You pick the corn. You bring it in to your store house. This is only the second stage for a farmer. First he sows the corn, then and just as importantly, he harvests the corn. Thirdly, he stores the corn. From his storage bins he sells it to processors and to markets. The stages of harvesting and selling a farmer's corn are just as important as sowing it and looking after it in the growth stage. Could you imagine a farmer sowing and not expecting a return, or could you imagine a farmer growing a crop and then letting it rot in the ground without even harvesting it? We are doing the same thing if we don't allow people to give to us. Have you ever tried to give somebody something nice and they won't take it?

I was given a beautiful car at a time when I needed a car. Some time later, I came across a person who needed a car. I still had this great car. By this time the car was ten years old but still a very reliable and well kept car. I went to the person privately and told them I had a car for them. The man said thanks but I have no money to pay for it as he had lost everything in a bad business partnership. I went on to explain that I just wanted to give him the car. I told him I would pay the transfer fee and that all he had to do was sign the transfer papers. I had even had the car detailed and filled the tank just to give it as best as I could.

The man would not accept the car, he refused point blank to take it. Not that I had to, but I even explained that the car had been given to me in a similar fashion and I was most happy for it to be a help to him in a time of need just as it was to me in my time of need. I left there with my car. I drove to that man so excited about giving it to him. All they way there I pictured his face, the happiness and excitement as he was given a car. But I drove it back home feeling most dejected. I hadn't lost anything but could you imagine buying somebody a lovely birthday present and them not accepting it. Even though this car had not actually cost me any thing, I wanted to help the man. I had learned how to live. I had learned to live by my giving and he needed to learn this principle more than anybody else I knew. He missed out on a lot more than just a car but why could he not receive? The man went on to lose all he had. I know of one other person who tried to help him but he would not accept anything from that person either. Why not? I can only imagine that his pride and lack of understanding stopped him from receiving that car from me. The last I heard of him, he was on the welfare system and going through a long phase of depression. Why did he take welfare payments from the government but not business tools from people trying to help?

This man was a business man; he had a good and sound business mind. But when his business partner stole all the money from the business account and left him with debts, he refused to get over it. This is a whole new subject in itself but the fact is, he just has to get over it. He placed too much importance on the money that was stolen from him and not enough importance on getting on with life.

I went through a similar experience when I set up a business with two other gentlemen who had nothing to start with. I paid them a wage and we set up a business. They ended up stealing all they could from me and I ended up with my house mortgaged and working two jobs to pay for it. I was very bitter toward those men and spent a lot more time thinking of ways to legally hurt them than ways of getting on with my life.

It wasn't until I met my friend Ken, who was an assistant to the rich Jew, that I was fortunate enough to have somebody to sit me down and explain that not only did I have to get on with my life but that I had to completely and totally, forgive those men who had stolen from me because, as long as was spending my time, my effort and most of all, my creative ability thinking about my ex-partners, then I would never be able to get on with and truly succeed in life and business, including my marriage and friendships. As long as I was dwelling on the past, I was a miserable person to be around and not going anywhere useful.

Just stop for a moment and think about the last person you know who was going through a divorce. Have you ever been around the person who just wants to tell you about how bad their divorce case is? Or how bad the break up of their business partnership is? These people are draining. They are terrible to be around. I'm not making light of divorce cases or the hardships of a partnership gone bad, but don't let these people suck the life blood out of you. As much as they need support, they also have to get over it and get on with life. Don't allow yourself to be stuck in conversation that is unproductive and eroding your creative and positive mentality.

It was a difficult task at first to forgive people who had deliberately deceived me and done me wrong. But as my friend Ken explained, until I totally forgave them, including speaking well of them, I would never be able to succeed as I should in business or other relationships. Did you notice that when I first referred to the men I referred to them as gentlemen? This is a deliberate way of speaking about such people. Ken pointed out that instead of calling them all sorts of names every time I referred to them, I was only doing myself harm. Until I began speaking well of them and only saying good things about them I had not totally forgiven them and, ultimately, this is a very important part of the Jewish wealth system. Forgiving people and not holding animosity against them is a whole subject in itself. My goal here is to inform you so that you are simply aware. From there it is up to you how much time and study you put into these principles. An interesting fact, proven scientifically, has shown that being unforgiving is directly related to sickness.

When you give, do not give publicly but give in private. The Jewish law says that when you give to charity, do not let your left hand know what your right hand is doing. In the case of the car I was trying to give, I had arranged a time to meet the man for a coffee so that I would not embarrass him by having other people around. This is the principle of not letting your left hand know what your right hand is doing.

Many people give, but few people receive. It is one thing, and quite a hard thing to teach people to give, but it is a very much harder task to teach people to receive.

Giving is only the first part; receiving, once you have learned to give is just as important. Remember, receiving is just as important as giving. When you give, expect to receive. When will you receive? Look back at the farmer and his process of sowing and reaping. Everything will produce in its due season.

Giving is only the first part, receiving, once you have learned to give is just as important.

Who do you give to?

As mentioned earlier, who you give to is as important as the habit of giving itself. You know to give serious consideration to the organisation or the individual you intend giving to. It is important to ensure that you are not funding their poverty and bank rolling them to the next handout; rather, you are giving either as a means to an end or giving to those who are making a difference and being a part of that infinite difference.

The idea of giving ten percent of your earnings has long been associated with that of the religious church. On one hand it is absolutely correct to give to an organisation such as a church, who is seeing to the larger picture of making life better for those in need and financially assisting and paying the wage of those who choose to do this work as their livelihood. But on the other hand, you must do your due diligence just as you would with any other organisation and see it the same way as the farmer making an investment in the soil he chooses to plant his seed.

History lesson

Let's look at the history of the Jewish church. In western civilisation, the church has long been known as being poor. This was not always the case and certainly never the case with the Jewish church.

Historically the Jewish church has always been very rich. It is the western society church and European church belief systems that have put a poverty mentality into the religious cords of the church community.

Throughout the history of the Jewish church, taking a vow of poverty was not only wrong but against the law. It was and is against the Jewish law because it goes against all that the law stands for. The richest men in history were Jews, as was the richest church building in history - Solomon's temple. Solomon's wealth still intrigues every treasure hunter and story writer who has read about the wealth of the man. The temple he built is well recorded as being overlaid with gold and the conundrum of silver being considered worthless due to the vast amounts of gold he used throughout his city of Jerusalem. Therefore, the idea of a church being poor was, until much later in history, never given consideration.

This book was not written to condemn any particular church and your own research into the history of the church and its associated religion will reveal the time and reason that poverty, as a symbol of humility, was introduced. The Jewish church was the richest church in history, ever. Again, if you are interested in researching the Jewish church and the original temple, full plans, weight of the gold used and the value of the gold and other material, is all recorded in public archives.

The idea of a church being poor was, until much later in history, never given consideration.

Employment and business

The Jewish law clearly states that you are to work. On top of this, ideally you are to be in a position of charge, a position of authority; a position of directorship. In other words, you are to be the boss.

As the boss or CEO of a company there will be times when you must discipline a subordinate. Understand that you are only to go so far, do not over do it to a point where the person is degraded. The Jewish law states the person is not to be treated as an animal.

"You shall not muzzle an ox when he treads out the grain". This is an interesting extract of the Jewish law. For example, let the workers of a process line eat that on which they work. Everybody has heard of the typical chocolate factory assembly line where people can eat while they work - after a day or two they don't touch it anyway. Learn not to be stingy with your workers, give them part, of or the left over parts of the produce, or set up a staff discount on products that you produce. Allow the staff to benefit from the profit in other ways than the normal remuneration of agreed wages.

When you are dealing with other people in business, learn not to begrudge a man his profit. Many people seem to have the idea that they always have to crunch everybody on every deal and that it's just good business practice. This is not always the case. Remember that he is in business just as you are, remember also that you reap what you sow. Therefore, if you are always crunching every deal to a point where the other person is barely making a profit, don't complain when your boomerang comes back. Don't complain that business is tough out there if you're tough on everybody else. Why would you not want another person to prosper in business and make a profit?

If the last paragraph has made you mad or has got you questioning yourself as to who this author thinks he is; if you are thinking that he couldn't possibly be in business for himself, then stop and take a moment to think about your last deals. Think about how you have been treated and how you have treated others in business. The boomerang comes back! You reap what you sow. The scales balance.

You must not use false weights or measuring instruments in your business.

You must ensure that the calculation and measuring instruments you use for the sale of your products are accurate. For example, if you own a service station, you must ensure that the fuel pump reads correctly so that you do not overcharge.

The Jewish law of prosperity states that correct measuring instruments will not only make you wealthy but that you will live longer. In this lays a very interesting point that's worth researching at a later stage.

Can you see the underlying backbone of the law? A system built around morals, integrity and honesty. Many cultures refer to the above as karma or cause and effect or simply 'what goes around comes around'. The fact is, that just as the farmer referred to earlier, you will always reap what you sow. If you steal from people, you will be stolen from. If you charge too much for a product or service, you will get charged too much when you come to buy. It is a universal and mostly well understood law of the unseen world, whether you call it merry-go-rounds and roundabouts, sowing and reaping, karma, what goes around comes around or any other terminology, the law is the same. Do to others that which you would want others to do to you. Note the positive slant on the last sentence; it does not state that you should not do something to somebody, thereby avoiding a bad thing being done in return, but the positive slant of instigating a positive action and thereby receiving positive reactions and favourable results.

When you are dealing with other people in business, learn not to begrudge a man his profit.

Principles of the Jewish wealth

Speaking and the importance of what you say

The words you speak have an enormous impact on your life, your business, your health and those around you.

Change the words you speak from the negative tense to the positive tense. Understand the importance of the way you think and speak. For anybody who has had any form of success training or who has read any success material this will be obvious and not a difficult concept to understand. But if you have never had explained the importance of deliberately watching the words you speak, this is an extremely important chapter that you may need to re-read time and time again.

Have you ever noticed that people who always say they are sick are always sick? Understand the power and strength of the words you speak. You must erase from your vocabulary dogmatic statements that you say daily or regularly in relation to any negative situation. For example, have you heard a person sneeze and then make the dogmatic statement of "I must be coming down with a cold"? Stop and think of the words you are speaking that have negative connotations. Guard your tongue and the words you say like a savage dog guarding its territory. Don't allow the dogmatic statements that were most likely passed on to you by your parents and friends be a part of your language. Just as important is to correct people when they say negative things about you. When you sneeze and somebody tries to "label" you as being sick, turn and correct them by saying "Oh no. I have the greatest immune system known to man-kind!" This may feel strange at first but only because you have been taught to speak and see in the negative realm instead of the positive.

If this concept of the power of guarding your words is new to you then you must invest in books and other success material explaining the power of positive speech.

The Jewish law strictly forbids a Jewish person to speak of themself as being sick or poor. Why? Because of the power of the words you speak. You eventually become exactly that of which you think and say about yourself.

To summarise on this, be very careful of the dogmatic statements that you say daily and regularly because the way you think, and in turn the way you speak, have a direct impact on the course your life will take. You must remove from you vocabulary statements such as "I can't afford it". Rephrase such an expression if you need to but don't allow the thoughts of not being able to afford something sink down into your subconscious mind. Why say that you can't afford something? Whose business is it if you don't have the money for it? Why not just say no, not today and leave it at that. You haven't lied but you haven't sunk the negativity of poverty into your subconscious mind either.

You all too often you hear people speaking to their car, they speak to whatever they are working on. What do you most likely hear somebody say when the car won't start? "This stupid car is always breaking down, it'll never start". That almost sounds normal if you have not been re-educated in how to think and speak. How often do you hear people telling the computer how stupid it is? But turn that around and speak in the positive sense. Is the only difference between the human race and any other that we can speak? Then why abuse it. Speak well to your investments, speak well at your donations and speak well of your business. When somebody asks how your day is going, there is no need to tell them of the stress and hardships you may be experiencing. Why can't you change your dogmatic statements to "Every day is a good day"?

An old saying:
You become what you think of most of the time.

This could be a whole new book in it-self. A book well worth reading is "Think and grow rich" by Napoleon Hill. It was originally written in 1938 and has been re-printed many times. Most of what he says in his book regarding the way you think has come straight out of the Jews law on life. He reiterates the importance of not only speaking positively but thinking positively. To quote Napoleon Hill - "You become what you think of most of the time". This is a direct translation from the Hebrew story of a wealthy man who became the victim of circumstances that he thought about most of the time. The man said, "The thing I have feared most has come upon me". Did you notice that it never said he was in a bad situation until he dwelled upon and worried about being in a bad situation?

Remember every day is a new day, a new day to start things correctly. To quote Napoleon Hill, who was quoting a Jew - "As a man thinks, so is he". Stop reading for a moment and think about that. You are now at the point where you have been expecting to see yourself most of the time.

As a man thinks, so is he.
Napoleon Hill

When does it come back to you?

When does all this that you have given come back to you? When, and how, does the money you have given to charitable donations, the time you have given to those in need, and the value you have added to a person's life all come back? In a nut shell, it all comes in its season. Go back to the farmer. The farmer expects a return, he expects a harvest on that which he has sown but, when does it come? When does his harvest come? It comes in its due season. Everything has a season. All things work in cycles of season according to what, where and how it was sown.

An interesting point is that a farmer has to first sow his seed before he can even think about getting any return. If you think that you can just try the idea out and give away one thing once then you are wasting your time, money and effort. When a farmer sows seed, he just keeps on sowing and planting. He doesn't sow one seed or just one kernel of corn and watch it and say that the whole idea just doesn't work. He doesn't go out into the field, dig out the seed and check if it is growing. He goes on about his business. He goes on about sowing in other fields and harvesting what he planted in a different season. This is the same mentality that you are to have when expecting a return on what you have given; just keep giving it out. Remember, everything matures and grows in its due season.

Principles of the Jewish wealth

How does it come back?

Many people ask me how it all comes back. The fact is this, the universal law of the unseen realm ensures that it comes back to you in abundance and in much more than what you have put out, just as the law of gravity works in the unseen realm to stop you floating up to the ceiling. I spoke earlier of a car that I was given. It was a good car that could have been easily sold on the open market, but why was it given to me? The person did not owe me anything, he just heard through somebody else that I would soon need a car and he had a car that he would not need. Two important notes here – one: I did not go around asking people to give me a car. I went about my daily life doing my best to live the way that I had been taught about for the previous six months when I was asked to come to this mans house who had the car in the drive-way, cleaned and detailed just as you would to sell it. He gave me the car because he had found out that I had to sell my car and would be looking for a car. Point two: he was consciously looking to help somebody, he saw a need and knew he had the requirement to fill it. It's worth noting that the car I had I needed to sell because it was mortgaged and, due to the business partners that I was in business with, I could no longer make the payments on it. The car I was given was obviously debt free which brings us into a whole new arena of the principles of the Jewish wealth system.

Get out of debt

If the idea of giving was a bit much for you to swallow, then hang on to your seat because the next law may seem impossible at first for you to grasp.

The Jewish law states that you are not to owe anybody any money. You may have heard of the strange way that Jews lend money. Generally they do not lend to their own people but only to other nationalities. The way they lend to their own people is a strange system of not charging interest because of the seriousness of the Jewish law. Can you imagine doing business without borrowing money? Come across to the positive side before you say that I don't know your business, before you tell me you're a property developer and how could I expect anybody to carry on business without borrowed funds. Think first of all about the positives. Think of all the media coverage when an interest rate rise is on the horizon. Put yourself in the position of your current business, your current employment and your current home but without a mortgage, without a car and equipment lease and without an overdraft. Now realign your thinking to other ways of building that business without the thought of borrowing money. If the concept is too hard to imagine then keep imagining because the way of the Jew is to stay out of debt. The Jewish law states that a Jew is to be the lender and not the borrower. Now, when you tell me that you can't do business without borrowed funds, think again. Tell me, where did those borrowed funds come from? Stop and think about it. While you are paying interest, somebody else is getting paid interest on their investment. That's their form of employment. That's their form of investment. They have lent you the money to do that development, they have lent you the money to buy that house, that car, to carry on that business.

As a lender you are in a position of power. When you now hear on the nightly news that a rate rise is on the horizon you get excited instead of being filled with fear as so many others are. They now have to work harder and longer hours to make those repayments but you, you just got a pay rise! You just got your employee, your money, working harder and giving you an even better return on your investment.

That's the law of the Jew. Be the lender and not the borrower. Why do you think that the law has been alive for so many years but kept a strict Jewish secret? Somebody has to borrow the money so that the Jew can be the lender.

Start thinking in terms of paying cash for your next car. If that means using the same car for another year or two, so be it, Saving the money for two years is a lot cheaper than making repayments on it when the majority of what you pay is just the interest. Sit down and do the calculations on what it costs to borrow money for your house. Most house mortgages are set over a thirty year period. A simple way to work out how much of the principle you are paying and how much is eaten up in interest, is to stop and do the following calculation. Take the amount you owe on your home loan. I will use an example of three hundred thousand dollars as it is the average amount borrowed for an Australian home loan at the time of writing. The repayments on three hundred thousand dollars, at the current rate of seven and a half percent are; two thousand and ninety eight dollars a month. Now take the rate of seven and a half percent and multiply it by the amount you have borrowed, the three hundred thousand. This is the amount of interest you are paying each year on the principle amount of three hundred thousand. This amounts to twenty-two thousand, five hundred dollars. Now divide this by twelve months to get a monthly figure - one thousand, eight hundred and seventy-five dollars. Therefore, only two hundred and twenty three dollars of the two thousand and ninety eight dollars a month you are paying goes to paying back the loan.

Now work that backwards by putting that same two thousand and ninety eight dollars a month into a savings account earning you six percent interest. That is, a percent and a half below the mortgage rate. The same compounding effect of repaying two and a half times back the amount borrowed will work for you in the positive sense of saving the money. You will have saved three hundred thousand dollars in just less than nine years.

The Jewish law states that putting your money in the bank is the smallest investment you can make; it says you are to work your money. It says you are in fact to trade. It says the least thing you can do is to put your money in the bank and earn interest. This is actually considered lazy.

The Jewish law says you are to work your money.

Types of business

Study what types of business Jews are associated with. Jews are generally traders, they buy and sell. In all aspects of life, including business, make it a priority to search for wisdom, understanding and knowledge. The Jew is a hard worker but not working hard. He runs his business, he is in control of his business but he is not required to be there nine to five. This is a broad statement but the outlines don't change. How can you have several businesses if you need to be in each one nine to five? When you have your business running well, train and employ a manager and start another business, open another branch and so on.

Find yourself a Jew in business and start asking questions.

Paying taxes

Pay your taxes. Don't get caught up in scams, schemes and ways of trying to avoid paying tax. By all means be diligent in minimising the amount you are paying but understand that you are under a legal obligation to pay your taxes as part of giving back to the wider community. The Jewish law of wealth states very clearly that you are to pay your taxes to whom taxes are due and to pay respect to whom respect is due.

When will the wealth come?

Don't be anxious for your wealth, it will come. Don't worry about daily life.

The Jew (law) asks, who by worrying and being anxious can add one unit of measure to his stature or to the span of his life?

It is unhealthy to worry. Learn to manage the stress of life and business. While studying for my helicopter license, I was intrigued to learn that stress management is directly related to physical fitness. Basically, the more stress you undertake, the more physical fitness you must include. Therefore, stress can cause sickness. Stay fit, stay healthy; don't worry. Remember the farmer, he plants, sows and expects a harvest because he firmly believes that all things have a due season.

Don't hold a grudge

Get over it. As mentioned earlier, my friend Ken had to be very blunt with me when he explained that not only did I have to get over the people who had stolen from me that I had been in business with, but that I had to completely forgive them. The same is true for a broken marriage, bad business partners and bad experiences.

These things will stop you from moving ahead in life if you don't forgive people and get over it. By holding a grudge or having animosity in your life you will be destroying all other areas of life. You cannot focus and be a creative business mind while holding on to animosity. You can't move forward in relationships and in your giving if you are allowing yourself to be hurt by past experiences. These things hold you back. You can certainly learn from bad experiences but not moving forward after a bad experience means that you have not learned from it at all.

My friend Ken had to be very blunt with me when he explained that not only did I have to get over the people who had stolen from me that I had been in business with but that I had to completely forgive them.

The saying of money being the root of all evil

The Jewish law concerning the above statement is well know and has been miss-quoted by people for many years (usually by poor people).

The Jewish law translated states; "The love of money is the root of all evil".

Do you notice the difference? When you read the correct translation of the statement and the idea that is thrown around, there is a huge difference.

It does not say "money is the root of all evil" it says "the love of money is the root of all evil". In other words, if you love money, firstly you will never be able to give it away. Secondly, if you love money it will control you instead of you controlling it. This is a very important area to understand. Money is our servant; we are not to be a servant to our money. If you have lost money in a business deal, in a divorce or any other situation then GET OVER IT.

If you can't get over it regardless of the amount, then you have a love of money. The money that you have lost is controlling you and it will ruin your life, you will be consumed by it.

Whether you have money or not, if you have a love of money, you will do anything to get it. You will deal illegally, you will deal without morals, and you will deal without thought of repercussions. These actions will bring about total loss, loss of health, loss of freedom and, ultimately, loss of life itself.

Being able to give money away proves you are in control of your money. If you can't give money away, then it is controlling you. Sure enough, the love of money is the root of all evil.

The principles of the Jewish law are a lifestyle. Being wealthy is not a case of chasing money but a case of money chasing you. The principles work. Whether or not you believe in the principles is the same as whether or not you believe in gravity, gravity is at work around you all the time. You can fight the laws of gravity or you can accept that the laws of gravity exist and choose to work within those laws and make gravity your servant, make gravity work for you instead of working against you. Make the laws of gravity a lifestyle, learn all you can about the laws of gravity, be it through education or by trial and error, but learn.

While I was studying to fly, we were taught a brief history on the research and development that went into making a machine fly. Designers did not design an airplane to create new laws but they designed a machine to fly within the unseen laws of the universe. The principles of flight are mathematical and carefully calculated to make the airplane a safe, reliable piece of equipment that can be perfectly and accurately manipulated with ease. The helicopter is a brilliant example of engineering that came from much trial and error, trial and error of working with existing laws and not trying to change the laws of gravity.

Return on investment

The Jewish law states the return on investment to be expected when you give. You may feel strange or uncomfortable about giving to receive but when you understand the principles of the law at work, you will understand that, like the laws of gravity, when you give, you will receive. You must position yourself to receive and expect to receive. This is not pie in the sky theory but proven and calculated.

The law states exactly how much to expect in return when giving charitable gifts; there is a lot to understand.

Basically you must research the charity that you are giving to, you don't just give to the first person who puts out their hand. Go back to the farmer again who studies the best ground in which to sow his seed. He deliberately and carefully sows his investment. He looks over that seed until he has a harvest. He expects a harvest, he expects a return and he expects to get a lot more back than what he sowed in the field.

As the Jewish law says to expect between thirty times and one hundred times the amount you have put out, you know what to expect in return. The amount the farmer gets back depends on the type of soil he planted his seed in. But the important note is this; he expects a return. A return much larger than the one he planted.

Remember the kernel of corn; the kernel has to be planted, it has to be given to the soil. From there it is broken down but it produces many stalks, each with many cobs, and each with many, many kernels. So what if one of those kernels is a dud, what if one doesn't produce a return, a harvest? Don't worry about it; you have planted so much that it will be surrounded by all the other good seeds you planted.

What to give
Again, the Jewish law gives example after example using exact and practical illustrations to tell us how to give, when to give, what to give, how much to give and who to give to. Let's briefly summarize.

How?
Giving of your finances is only one part of giving. You give of your time to worthy causes, you give of your resources and you give of your abilities.

When?
First fruits: the first thing you do before you pay bills is to set aside your gift to charity. Once you have the mentality of giving as being the most important part of business life, you will make your giving the first thing you do. This is why the Jewish law says your giving is to be from the first fruits of your harvest.

What?
Ten percent of what you earn is the minimum you are to give according to strict Jewish law. If ten percent sounds like a lot to give then get started where you can. But make it a certain amount with the goal of increasing it. Start at five or two percent of your income, with goals of increasing at certain dates.

Who to give to?

The answer is worthy causes who are trying to help themselves. Don't fund another person's poverty, sow into good soil, and research your soil. Complete your due diligence just as you would any other company in which you are investing. Research who you are giving to and what they are doing with the money. How often does this person or organisation require help? In the case of an individual, are they trying to help themselves? If it is a charity organisation, what have they done with past donations? What programs do they have in place? How are they adding value to the lives of other people and the community at large?

Who don't you give to? You watch to make sure that you don't give for the wrong reasons. You don't give in order to obtain favour with the person. That's a bribe. You don't give to a friend who will then feel obliged that he must give directly back to you. That's trying to buy something. Remember that you are sowing a seed, not buying a product or service.

Giving a meal

This is a huge subject; it involves a lot more than just giving a meal or feeding a poor person. When you give, that is one thing. But when you go without to give, that brings us into a whole new area of giving. It is one thing to give of your abundance but to give when it means you then go without is a much bigger gift. The Jewish law directs to give a meal and you, yourself going without; and to do this on a regular basis. The terminology is the same as that used today by athletes and the like who understand the benefits to the human body from fasting.

Fasting is understood today as simply deciding to miss a meal or to miss solid foods for a day or more in order to cleanse the body. The Jew was directed to this but to give the meal which he was missing out on. This is a two-fold benefit: one as a natural form of cleaning out the body's digestive system and two, you are bringing your giving to a higher level.

Moving along

Don't stay angry. Get angry by all means, use anger as a tool. But don't go to sleep angry when you go to bed. Learn to use your emotions to your advantage. Most things that happen are a matter of perspective. Most things depend on how you view them.

Be careful how you live, live like a wise person,
Don't live like ignorant people, but like wise people. Make good of every opportunity you have.

Attitude

Most people reading this book would have had some form of success teaching, or at least read material covering the importance of the words you speak, the things you do and as importantly, the attitude you hold.

My friend Ken taught me the process from the words that I speak up to the point where I am in life today. Everything has a process, everything has a life cycle. If you are considering the idea of starting a family you don't just walk into the hospital one day and say you're there to have a baby, deliver it doctor. The doctor will laugh and tell you there's no baby in there. You plan to start a family. You prepare yourselves and your environment, you plant a seed, you nurture and care for that seed as it grows. You protect the environment that it is in. Your attitude toward that seed is one of care and responsibility. You speak kind and positive words toward it. Your emotions and the way you think are happy, positive and an expectation of a happy child. You make decisions regarding the child you are expecting, you take positive actions toward that child's birth.

You need to understand that the words you use in everyday conversation determine the way you think and feel. Your feelings or emotions have a huge impact on the daily decisions you make. Your decisions form the mold of your daily habits. The things you are doing every day are what build your character. And ultimately, it is your character that has you where you are today.

You must make your daily habits positive and deliberate. Don't allow negative words to come out of your mouth. The Jews have an interesting illustration of a large ship being controlled by a small rudder. The pilot in control of that small rudder determines the destiny of that huge ship and all who are on it. They also use the illustration of a horse being controlled by a small bit in its mouth. But, the illustration asks who can control the tongue of a human? For it has the power to cause good or harm.

Any form of success starts with attitude.

Shortcuts to the Jewish wealth

There are no shortcuts to the Jewish wealth, the principles remain unchanged. Just as the principles of flight were there before man learned how to use them to his advantage. Just as the laws of gravity have always been in place, so are the laws of the farmer and so are the laws of the principles of the Jewish wealth.

Slowly but surely, bit by bit, things start to happen. Coincidences move in your favour instead of against you. The principles of the Jewish wealth don't change your life overnight because you didn't get where you are overnight. It took time and decisions. Stick with what you have learned. Look at a vineyard; look at how long it takes for a vineyard to produce good wine. Many years of planting, watering, pruning and fertilising go into a vineyard before it produces the fruit for wine. But once it is established, once it is producing, the time spent in the scheme of things is irrelevant. In ten years from now you will look back and it will seem like no time since you wondered how you would change your circumstances.

When Ken first began to teach me about the principles to live by, I was still in debt, I still had bills past their due date but I changed my attitude. I believed in the principles and began working them to my advantage. I began making regular donations, I began to keep a look-out for those in need and, before long, I was meeting the needs of people that were larger than the needs I had when I first started out with the principles.

I met a young mechanic who was doing very well in business; everything seemed to go his way. I asked him what his secret to business was and he told me he didn't know. As I got to know him I understood he was applying all the principles of the

Jewish wealth out of habit. He didn't understand how or why it worked but it was his lifestyle taught to him by his dad. It was the integrity he was bought up with. He was honest in business, he was a giver, as far as I could see he was always happy and always ready to help out. He was unwittingly working the principles to his advantage, unlike so many other people who unwittingly work the principles against themselves.

The principles of the Jewish wealth are not some sort of principles that I have made up myself; I didn't discover them or put them together, I'm just sharing them. They were taught to me as they are taught to the Jews from a young age. Like a person who is born into great wealth, they don't know any different.

I have deliberately not included a hall of fame list of famous Jewish people who have won Nobel prizes, shaped modern history or built well known businesses. If your interest is with such people, the literature is readily available.

I have also avoided the political, religious and ethnic perspectives as much as possible because I was not taught the principles by a Jew. I was taught by a non-Jew who was introduced to the old Jew after being taught to live by the principles of the Jewish wealth. I have not discovered any of the material written in this book, I have just been the fortunate one to be entrusted with publishing the knowledge.

Putting it all together

The wealth of the Jews is just like the seed of a tree, it is already within you. Everything that a tree will be when it is mature is already inside the seed of that tree.
You need to believe in what you do and stand fast with what you believe. Consider the following points:

*   Know that the wealth of the world belongs to you. If you are a giver of wealth then you will be a receiver of wealth.

*   Understand the stages and the maturing process. Think back to the farmer and his corn. First comes the blade, then the ear, then the full corn in the ear. Don't pick the corn when it is just a small blade. You don't plant a seed and give up the next day because you haven't seen a result. Don't give up when you see that the corn is just a seedling either. Remember all that you plant has a life cycle, it has a season and a time that must pass before it can mature. Time must pass before you get a result and before you can eat and enjoy what you have planted.

*   Learn about giving a seed in relation to a need. Diligently seek a need that you can fulfill. If you want a new car, find somebody that needs a car and help them fulfill their dream as a part of fulfilling your own.

*   Understand the importance and benefits of being the lender and not the borrower. How many private money lenders are Jews?

*   No matter what you are or where you are in life, start now. It's never too late or too soon to apply the principles.

*   Don't be lazy; be involved in what goes on around you, don't be slack. Get involved in your investments. Be involved with your work or business by showing initiative. Become involved in your local community; involved with politics if the need be.

*   Be aware of what might be holding you back. Don't allow the negativity of people who don't believe stop you from being where you are supposed to be. Don't be drawn down to another person's level but find people who will lift you up to their level.

*   You must be driven; if you are not driven you will just drift. Understand that you are in control of your own destiny. Be fully devoted to what you do. Give your everything.

*   Know without a doubt that you are to succeed, know that you are to be prosperous and that you are to be wealthy. Remember that the Principles of the Jewish Wealth have been deliberately hidden for almost four thousand years. Why? To hide them from the lazy and the wicked. Every person in their right and conscious mind has the ability to attain wealth.

For reasons that we mostly misunderstand in Western culture, these principles of the Jewish wealth system were to be kept secret; they were strictly to be taught only to the children of the Jews. That is the Jewish culture.

Throughout history the Jewish race has been persecuted with such a passion because they succeeded and controlled the wealth of the world without even having a country to control it from. Just dwell on that and think about it for a moment; think about the Jewish people who lost everything in the holocaust including their parents, family, inheritance and all possessions and a few years after the war, they were back to running businesses and controlling major wealth.

Can you see the underlying or subliminal attitude of the principles of the Jewish wealth system? They are principles of honesty, integrity and forgiveness. Can you see yet that this is a lifestyle and not just a set of rules?

The principles are not new, they are not tricks or selling techniques or conniving ways of convincing a buyer to purchase but a lifestyle built on a solid foundation of long term integrity, even in the face of adversity, even when somebody else has tried to con you, you stand fast to what you know in your conscience is right. You know in your subconscious mind what will bring you through and prosper you time and time again. These are the principles of the system of attracting, attaining and maintaining wealth. These are the laws that will bring you to your rightful place in history, these are the principles that you are to teach your children and pass down the line.

You must be driven; if you are not driven you will just drift. Understand that you are in control of your own destiny. Be fully devoted to what you do. Give your everything.

Interesting points on Jewish lifestyle

Why do the Jews have laws such as not eating pork – Health is the foremost reason. The Jew is instructed to live a clean life, strictly hygienic physically, sexually and morally. The Jewish law has some very distinct and exact directions of what not to do as well as what to do, some are listed briefly;

Don't move your neighbor's boundary markers.
Don't take advantage of disadvantaged people
Honor you parents – deliberately
Don't get caught up in things like worshiping the sun, the moon, the stars or other objects, (this does not translate so obviously in western culture.)
Don't take bribes
Don't pervert justice.

Enough said, I would say the above laws speak for themselves!

Keeping a record.

For your own self, it is interesting to keep a record of what you have given and what you have received. I always find it so interesting to look back at when I was going through hard times but kept on giving, then to look at the truly amazing reception of wealth being bestowed on my life.

This book is only an introduction to the Jewish System of wealth and living, it is now up to you to be armed and qualified to diligently seek out all you can to

As I began to succeed in my life of giving and my world was beginning to turn around, I could see that I didn't understand all that I should. I tried to live by the principles taught to me as best as I could, however, my attitude still needed work. I still had that old mentality deep inside. To point this out, my friend Ken walked me through what he called an attitude test.
What could be an attitude test? I asked. Ken had noticed that I was always complaining about the cost of fuel. As he said, you can't do anything about the cost so why complain. By complaining you are telling yourself that you can't afford it. By putting in only a couple of dollars at a time in case it came down in price I was operating like a poor person, even though I had money in the

bank. Ken asked me did I ever take the little packets of salt and pepper from fast food outlets. In fact I did. I would take an extra couple of those little packets of salt that you get for your chips. I never had a use for an extra couple of packets but in the back of my mind I was keeping some for a rainy day. I was unwittingly planning to have a day so bad that I couldn't buy salt. In addition Ken pointed out that I was actually stealing the salt. That's going a bit far to call me a thief for taking extra packets of salt from the fast food and after all they are free! Aren't they? Well they are free while you are eating their food in their restaurant. But they were not put there for you to stock pile at home. Ken said "Once you understand this principle, you are well on your way". He followed by asking about government welfare and if I thought I deserved to be looked after by the government in my old age. By now I understood that it is not the government's job to look after me in my old age. People have come to expect that just because they are old or just because they can't find work that the government will arrange welfare for you. The concept of receiving welfare at any stage should not be a consideration for you. The government can't take good care of you because it was never their job to take care of you in retirement or before.

I remember what the old Jew said, "As a man thinks so is he, be it according to your faith". How big can you think? He asked me. I have learned to think for big things. I learned to understand that if I couldn't see myself flying my own helicopter that I would never have come to the place of owning it. He told me "Don't trust in your money, trust in your giving.

Speak positively about your life, your health, your donations and your business. Don't allow other people to speak negatively about you". Those words have stuck with me in all that I do.

For those people who have been raised in poverty, they will have a poverty mentality. This is a fair statement and such people should be given time and encouragement to develop in the principles described through out this book. These people who have had a poverty mentality instilled in them as a child would be expected to have the most difficulty in understanding the concepts involved in the principles of attracting wealth. Having an understanding you will recognize this scenario; How often have you been in the supermarket and you hear a child ask their parent for something? The parent (with out even stopping to think) says no because they can't afford it. This lazy response is putting a poverty mentality into that child at an early age. This mentality goes deep into the child's inner person and can be very hard to break.

Another group can be even more difficult to change the perception through which they see themselves. These are people who have some money, the people who have inherited, won or simply saved every dollar. They generally don't believe they could ever generate that physical money again and therefore they don't spend it. They have prosperity in their bank account but poverty in their spirit.

Ignorance of the law.

Ignorance of any law is never an excuse. It has been said, Imagine a person who has grown up in Amsterdam where they can almost do as they feel in relation to drugs that are illegal in most other nations. That person then inters a country where the death penalty applies for the possession of drugs. When that person is picked up and awaits his sentence, nobody gives a second thought as he cries and pleads ignorance of the law. Worse still, the law is written in another language, the law has never been explained to him, He has never been exposed to the idea of drugs being illegal. This is all new to him and before he knows it, he is waiting in a small and dirty cell, waiting to be executed.

The same applies to the laws of prosperity and the principles of wealth. Ignorance is no excuse, the laws still exist. The laws of gravity exist whether you know about it or not and whether you use it your advantage or not. The laws of other countries exist whether or not you research them before you enter that country and enjoy your time, enjoy the economy of that country and benefits of the produce is entirely up to you. No body will force you to benefit from another nations economy and the value of their currency in comparison to your own. You need to research and understand for your self the conversion of currency and the true cost of a product.

In the same way, it is you who needs to research the physical laws that affect the unseen realm.

Living out the principles is a lifestyle choice. In the same way as your health is a lifestyle choice. Do you just try being healthy for a couple of days or weeks? No, being healthy is lifestyle which may take time to show the benefits.

The food you eat to day will have an effect on you for many years to come. The difference is a healthy life style. A diet that lasts three weeks where you eat healthy food will have no good long term benefit. A healthy lifestyle of healthy habits and a majority of whole grain foods, fresh and unprocessed fruit and vegetables and lean meats will need to be a habit of healthy living. The principles are also a habit of healthy living. As a healthy diet is an ongoing pursuit that will grow in benefits over time, you need to understand that if you have an unhealthy diet then it will take time and discipline to change that lifestyle. Understanding and operating in the principles of wealth is a lifestyle in the same way as a healthy diet, a one off contribution to a charity will have no long term benefit. It is a case of making the principles of health and the principles of wealth a habitual lifestyle. Start today, whether it is your health or your wealth that is in need of a change of diet, the time to start is now. You may not see the benefits immediately but it's better to be healthy and wealthy in a couple of years from now due to the choices you make today.

Every person in their right and conscious mind has the ability to attain wealth. Remember that you can't have what you can't believe for. If an architect is to build an office block but he doesn't believe it will work out, how can he ever build it? Where would he start? If he doesn't believe it can be done, then he can never do it. But somebody else may come along with ideas or experience in that area and have the solution. He will build it because he believes it can be done.

If you can't see yourself being and enjoying wealth then you never will. You need to change your attitude, you need to dream. You have an imagination for a reason. Learn to use it.

It is unlikely that your job will bring you wealth directly. Look beyond your job, find a need and fill it. Your employer is not trying to make you rich, he is paying you the minimum that it takes to get you to come to work and do the job.

Signing for the package.

As we have covered in some detail, understand the power of the words you speak. Be certain to remove phrases such as "I can't afford it" and "I must be getting sick" from your vocabulary. Treat them as profanity. Take the approach and understanding that dogmatic statements of everyday life or "off the cuff" replies to unrelated circumstances are putting your subconscious mind in a negative connection with that of the unseen. Remember the power of the words you use have an effect far greater than what may have been meant. If you continue to use negative words in your ordinary conversation then don't complain when your words come to fruition, or when your harvest comes in because that is the seed you have been planting, that is the package you have just signed for.

Extrapolate the subliminal.

The Jewish law is often written in parables and stories. Through out their literature the question is asked why it is written in such a format.
The reason is given as hiding the principles from those who do not develop understanding (Understanding comes from study)
Wisdom comes from understanding and understanding from study.

The principles where hidden from the lazy. Lazy people where described as wicked and in some translations as evil.

The Jews have a very interesting story regarding business and wisdom called "The five talents of gold".
Now a talent was an old form of a measurement of weight. The exact weight of a talent is no longer known for sure however, it is known that a strong man could carry one talent but a talent was generally carried by two people.
For the sake of the story and to put this into perspective according to the ancient time it was written, being conservative a talent can be assumed as something around thirty kilograms or about sixty five pounds. (But in reality it may be a lot heavier) At a current price of around $US685 an ounce, that puts the value of a gold talent at something in the vicinity of US$712,400 in today's currency.

The Five talents of gold.

A man going off on an extended trip called his servants together and delegated responsibilities. To one he gave five talents, to another two talents and to the third he gave one talent, each depending on his ability. (Approximately $3,562,000 to the first, $1,424,800 to the second and $712,400 to the third) Then he left. Right off the first servant traded and doubled his master's investment. The second went out and worked, he to doubled his masters money. But the man with the single talent went out and dug a hole in the ground. He carefully buried his master's talent giving special consideration in his selection of a safe place to hide it.

After a long absence, the master of those three servants came back and settled up with them. The one to whom he had given the five talents proudly stepped forward and showed his master that he had doubled the money entrusted to him. His master commended him: "Good work!" he said, "You did your job well. From now on you will be my partner. I'll make you chief over five businesses".

The servant who was given the two talents showed how he had doubled his master's investment. His master commended him: "Good work! You did your job well, you have been wise with the small things so from now on, you'll be my partner and I'll make you chief over two businesses".

The servant given the one talent said, "Master, I know that you have high standards and hate careless ways, that you demand the best and make no allowances for error. I was afraid I might disappoint you, so I found a good hiding place and secured your money. Here it is, safe and sound down to the very last cent".

The master was furious. 'That's a terrible way to live! It's criminal to live cautiously like that! If you knew that I was after the best, why did you do less than the least? The least you could have done would have been to invest the sum with the bankers, where at least I would have gotten a little interest.

Take the talent and give it to the one who risked the most and now has ten talents. For everyone who has will be given more and he will have abundance. Whoever does not have, even what he has will be taken away from him. And get rid of this worthless "play-it-safe" servant who won't go out on a limb. Throw him out of my presence".

The story of the five talents was written thousands of years ago and still holds true today. With truly amazing insight and wisdom it clearly describes the results of both the seen and unseen at work in business life. Having been translated through many languages, the last paragraph still requires interpretation beyond that of the English language. The interpretation of wisdom and understanding that if you don't use what you are given then even what you have will be taken away. Another interesting point is that it was considered the least form of investing to put your money at interest with the bankers. The men who where commended and promoted both took risks. They both set about in business and made a 100% return in the time that the master was gone.

Let me go a step further, you work for your money and are then lazy with it by giving it to a funds manager to invest for example, in managed funds. You speak to your adviser once a year after that to be updated on the performance.

You have no control over that money and you have passed the responsibility on to someone else. Are you being lazy with your investments?

You may say "But I am to busy with my work to invest my money", So you put more time into earning new money than you do in building on and maintaining the money you already have!

Another story is written as a short parable written by King Solomon the richest man ever on record. "A little sleep, a little slumber, a little folding of the arms to rest and poverty will pounce on you, it will overtake you like an armed robber. He who has a slack hand becomes poor, but the hand of the diligent makes him rich.

He also wrote, "A rich mans wealth is his strong city; the destruction of the poor is their poverty".

Another of King Solomon's proverbs says,

Listen, friends, to some fatherly advice; sit up and pay attention so you'll know how to live. I'm giving you good council; don't ever forget this lesson. When I was a boy in my father's house, the pride and joy of my mother, He would sit me down and teach me. Take this to heart. Do what I tell you-live! Sell everything and buy wisdom! Forage for understanding!

Don't forget one word! Don't deviate or forget my words. Never walk away from wisdom- she guards your life; love her- she keeps her eye on you. Above all and before all, do this: Get wisdom! Write this at the top of you list: Get Understanding! Throw your arms around her- believe me, you won't regret it; never let her go- she'll make your life glorious. She'll garland your life with grace and present you with a crown of splendor. Listen my dear friend, take my advice and the years of your life will be many. I have taught you in the way of wisdom.

Another says "A little sleep, a little slumber, a little folding of the arms to rest and poverty will pounce on you like an armed robber, poverty will overtake you".

Being lazy at work will never make you wealthy.

Your employers' goal is not to make you wealthy.

Look at the person who inherits wealth but is not taught how to use it or how to apply the principles of gaining / maintaining wealth. The same is often as with the person who wins the lottery – so often they are back to where they where beforehand with in several years, why is this? Because they still have a poverty mentality, they have wealth on the outside but they are still poor on the inside, they don't know how they could ever do it again. Don't be lazy in your work, your business or your investments.

This book has introduced you to the Jewish system of wealth and living. It is now up to you to be armed and qualified to diligently seek out all you can.

It stands to reason that if you are always looking to help someone then you're never looking for trouble. You can't be saying kind words and mean words at the same time or planning good and bad for a person in the same thought. You can't be positive and negative simultaneously. Seek to be positively proactive. Seek to make life better for another person.

Never walk away from wisdom- she guards your life; love her- she keeps her eye on you. Above all and before all, do this: Get wisdom!

Notes

Principle
1   Giving, tithe, to the poor
2   Know that you are supposed to be wealthy
3   Be the lender and not the borrower
4   Be healthy
5   Don't steal, deal with integrity
6   Expect wealth, expect increase
7   Think and Speak and speak positively
8   Forgive
9   Believe, give and receive.

Expect big things…Believe big
Expect big, think big, look for better

Home work

Find yourself a Jewish person, buy them lunch and ask them to answer for the questions you have thought of while reading this

book.
Listed on the next page are some questions to get you started.

Questions for the Jew:

How did you learn this?
Were you taught?
Who taught you?
Do you tithe?
Do you give to charity?
Do you give on a percentage basis?
Are you strict about this?
Who do you give to? not as an individual but what type of person or group do you give to?
What type of business / businesses are you involved with
How did you get started?
Did you start the business your self?
What do you look for in a business?
What type of people do you look to deal with?
Are you in business for your self or do you work for somebody else?
Do you employ family members?
If so, how much of your business is made up of family members?
Do you have rules, / laws that you follow in relation to money / finance?
How many different businesses are you involved in?
Do you use debt / borrowed money in your business life?

Do you use debt / borrowed money in your personal life?

Do you use debt / borrowed money in your investments

Ask: What advice can you give to somebody who is not a Jew on the following topics?

Business

Finance

Personal life

What do you invest your money in?

Notes

_____
_____
_____
_____

www.ingramcontent.com/pod-product-compliance
Lightning Source LLC
Chambersburg PA
CBHW021859170526
45157CB00005B/1890